AF283098

© 2017 Prestel Verlag, Munich · London · New York, a member of
Verlagsgruppe Random House GmbH, Neumarkter Straße 28, 81673 Munich

© for the texts, Ross McGinnes, 2017, with the exception of the Foreword,
which is © Marina O'Loughlin, 2017
© for the images, see Contributors, p. 112, 2017

In respect to links in the book the Publisher expressly notes that no illegal content was
discernible on the linked sites at the time the links were created. The Publisher has no
influence at all over the current and future design, content or authorship of the linked
sites. For this reason the Publisher expressly disassociates itself from all content on
linked sites that has been altered since the link was created and assumes no liability
for such content.

Prestel Publishing Ltd.
14–17 Wells Street
London W1T 3PD

Prestel Publishing
900 Broadway, Suite 603
New York, NY 10003

Library of Congress Control Number is available; British Library
Cataloguing-in-Publication Data: a catalogue record for this book
is available from the British Library

Editorial direction: Lincoln Dexter
Copy-editing: Aimee Selby
Design: gradedesign.com
Production management: Friederike Schirge
Separations: Reproline Mediateam, Munich
Printing and binding: DZS Grafik d.o.o.
Paper: Profibulk

Printed in Bosnia and Herzegovina

MIX
Paper from
responsible sources
FSC® C110418

Verlagsgruppe Random House FSC® N001967

ISBN 978-3-7913-8428-3

www.prestel.com

CONTENTS

FOREWORD

BY MARINA O'LOUGHLIN, RESTAURANT CRITIC

To say I was startled when the bread arrived in a man's tweed flat cap is an understatement. Sure, I knew the cap was pristine, unworn – but I still couldn't shake the worrying notion that the bread tasted faintly of greasy scalp. Complete autosuggestion of course, but I don't think this was the impression that the much-lauded Yorkshire restaurant wanted to leave me with.

Eating in as many restaurants as I do, you tend to spot trends. Some are welcome, sure-fire indicators of a clued-up kitchen. Others not so much: I'm pretty confident in saying that if your coleslaw arrives in a mini supermarket shopping trolley, you are not in for any culinary fireworks.

Over the years I've been subjected to the kind of presentation devices that should never have left the chefs' crania: 'fine dining' joints where you're required to pluck morsels off bespoke metal sculptures that look like something dreamed up by the creators of the *Saw* franchise. Distracted by the 'artistry', it's only belatedly you realise that the monkfish beignet had all the appeal of a leftover fish finger. I've had sashimi draped over wine glasses and sushi on a plank, belching out a fug of dry ice. Take it from me, dry ice does sushi no favours.

I've drunk mango cocktails from fake milk cartons, the spout jammed with a Mini-Babybel. Seafood cocktails have arrived on top of glass bowls containing live fish. BBQ ribs on dustbin lids; casseroles in billycans. Cured ham hung from wire with clothes pegs, sauces in syringes. Endless numbers of rocks and cake stands and tree trunks. A recent high-end US meal involved a flurry of little starters laid out like a Japanese garden, all pebbles and moss.

But even the less actively insane serving vessels come with undeniable downsides. Have you ever tried pouring gravy over a roast presented on a chopping board? The result ain't pretty. Or the bizarre popularity of delivering food on slate, often not more evolved than basic roof

tiles. Here's what I wrote on this daftness after dinner at an ambitious hotel restaurant in Wales:

Many dishes arrive on slate. Dear God, enough with the slate: the screeching of the cutlery, the inability of the staff to clear tables with any kind of grace, the inevitable seepage and leakage. One dessert includes basil sorbet. Of course, it melts inexorably off its slate, creating an ectoplasmic mess on the tablecloth, as though it had been vomited on by Slimer from *Ghostbusters*.

I've not yet been to the Taiwanese restaurant that celebrates food's inevitable destination by serving it in little toilet bowls. I mean, why?

The arrival of Instagram has only intensified the lunacy. One thing I have learned, almost without exception: the more ludicrous the presentation, the worse the food – but hey, count those likes. And yes, I'm guilty as any of spreading the 'wisdom' on social media as anyone else. Back to that flat cap: bemused, I put a snap of it up on Twitter, and someone immediately replied tagging @WeWantPlates, my first introduction to an account that rapidly became a cult and even more rapidly a sensation. I loved what Ross was doing; this was a mission I could get behind. When presented with another piece of nonsense instead of regular crockery, we should all raise the battlecry: we want bloody plates.

INTRODUCTION

BY ROSS McGINNES

It all started when a friend posted this picture of his dinner on Facebook. It was captioned: 'That is a big meal!'

It wasn't a big meal. It was an average-sized meal served on a bloody huge chopping board. His steak, chips and weird Jenga salad could all have fitted perfectly on a nice white plate, but the restaurant seemingly didn't have any, or perhaps nobody had bothered to empty the dishwasher. My friend had fallen for the insidious trend of style-over-content gastropub guff.

When a restaurant serves food on a massive plank they can get away with charging you more. A Hipster Tax, if you like. The same goes for slates, which I think we can all agree belong on roofs, or beneath sheep on a Welsh hillside. Add a mini shopping trolley of chips (hand-cut and triple-cooked, naturally), bread in a handbag or drinks served in jam jars wrapped in hessian, and it'll get Instagrammed to boot. I was on to something.

A quick scan of Twitter hashtags like #bringbackplates revealed plenty of diners venting their irritation at the way their food was being served, but no account heading the crusade. @WeWantPlates was born, and two years later, after worldwide media coverage and with a quarter of a million followers on social media, our crockery crusade continues to gather strength. The 2015 John Lewis annual report even claimed 'the international We Want Plates social media movement helped spark a sales uplift of 18% in plain white dinner plate sales.' Mind you, we're still waiting for our complimentary dinner service as thanks.

So how did we arrive at this Hipstergeddon of plateless buffoonery?
The restaurant business is cut-throat and ultra-competitive, so in order to stay one step ahead of the competition, owners and chefs have to continually evolve and find new and exciting ways to entice customers.

Yet in recent times it's not the food that has evolved, more the presentation. With every diner armed with a camera on their phone, pictures are snapped and shared in seconds. There's currently a staggering 230,227,031 photos with the hashtag #food on Instagram – and another 300 have been added in the time it has taken you to read this sentence.

But when you look beyond all the unfathomable numbers and Instagram filters, has the food actually improved? Or are chefs spending so much time faffing around balancing chips in miniature wheelbarrows that the taste becomes secondary?

Allow me to illustrate using the example of my local pub, which used to do a great Sunday roast: twelve quid, piled high, tasted great – and yes, it came on a plate. One weekend they added a quirky offering to the menu: little sandwiches, pies, dainty cakes and mini milkshakes *served on a miniature picnic bench.* The benches, painted bright pink and yellow, sat on top of tables seating actual grown adults. And what was the first thing these infantilized diners did? It wasn't try the food – it was whip out their phones and take a picture. Over the following months the picnic benches became increasingly popular, coinciding with the specials board becoming progressively smaller, before it eventually disappeared altogether. I sat there one Sunday watching bench after garish bench emerge from the kitchen like a technicolour carnival of idiocy, before my usual roast arrived. The meat was cold, the spuds were burnt and you could've skimmed the Yorkshire pudding across a pond. It was once their main Sunday trade, but the traditional roast had died an unpalatable death.

But that's OK, because they were doing a roaring trade with the benches, right? Sure, until the pub down the road started doing them too. Then the one around the corner. Before you knew it, everyone was doing the same 'quirky' thing, except it wasn't 'quirky' any more because you couldn't move for mini picnic benches, and now all their roast dinners are crap to boot.

Moving on to the actual act of *eating* these creations. The next time you're pouring gravy onto a chopping board, take a moment to question the chef's sanity. Do any of us enjoy chasing blueberries around a roof tile covered in icing sugar, racing against time to eat the accompanying ice cream before it melts all over the table and onto our lap? How often do we reflect on 'that wonderful little restaurant we went to, where for dessert we had to extract fruit from a Newton's cradle and eat it with tweezers'?

Menus add to the confusion. If you're going to serve meals on manky old chopping boards, don't dress them up as 'organic woodland serving slabs'. 'Here you are sir, your artisanal homogeneous metamorphic platter.' 'Errr ... that's a slate, mate.' And when did '9.5' become a thing? Just write £9.50!

It's not just diners who suffer: spare a thought for the poor staff waiting tables. Usually on a small wage, they're at the mercy of the chef's monumental ego as they attempt to juggle great slabs of marble and driftwood across the restaurant without the life-sized ceramic rabbit or reproduction medieval sword falling off.

Here's an extract of an email we received from an exasperated waitress, who wished to remain anonymous, with the subject line: A Plateless Wasteland.

I don't have photos since I'm not allowed to use my phone while I'm on the clock, but I work at —— in ——.

The plateless horrors I've seen are innumerable. On our current menu we have mussels served in little cans, shrimp arranged on a chunk of driftwood and a chocolate bar hidden in some olive branches in a vase.

There is a dish served not on an ordinary board but a charred slice of log, and a tortilla and egg concoction served in a tiny skillet on top of a board, one side of which holds slices of steak draped over two beef rib bones.

You'd think that a restaurant so obsessed with putting wines in their correct glasses would pay a bit more attention to hygiene and stop trying so hard.

Just know that whenever you go to a restaurant with no plates, there is at least one staff member who thinks it's as dumb as you do.

Yours, ——

There are of course exceptions to the rule. A ploughman's lunch belongs on a board. Pizza boards are fine, because most pizzas are too big for a plate anyway. Steak stones allow you to cook your meat exactly as you like, while Himalayan salt blocks do a fine job of seasoning, although you do look like a bit of a pillock eating off one. A pint of prawns? Great. Not so a pint of chips, pint of sausage rolls, pint of bacon or pint of profiteroles. Yep, we've seen all those.

Oh, and sushi does what sushi wants. Sushi is above the law. In fact, if sushi *isn't* served in a wooden boat decorated with flowers and unpronounceable fruit, you should storm out in a theatrical huff.

Then there are the venues themselves. If you're lucky – or daft – enough to eat at some of the more left-field Michelin-starred restaurants, then you'll probably be disappointed if your seafood starter *doesn't* arrive on a scale model of the *Titanic* in a sea of dry ice as 'My Heart Will Go On' plays from an iPad hidden under the table.

See, We Want Plates isn't about having a pop at celebrity chefs who spend more time in front of the camera on *Saturday Kitchen* than they do in front of a stove. It's about the try-hards who take a perfectly normal dish and send it to the table in the most ridiculous fashion – usually with a hefty premium on the bill.

'Why no naming and shaming?' you cry. We do with chains, or big-hitters who can take it on the chin, but we're not out to hold small businesses up to ridicule. That is, apart from the Hereford coffee house that denied serving Scotch eggs in jelly moulds, despite being presented with photographic evidence from customers, leading to us being called 'plate Nazis' on the town's Facebook page. They were fair game.

Finally, a word on fact-checking. Images are submitted from around the globe; their provenance is checked, menus are viewed online and calls made to restaurants. Of the 2,000-plus pics shared on our Twitter, only one has been revealed as a fake. It was a ploughman's lunch on a table tennis bat. Though seeing as we'd already verified four other meals on table tennis bats, I hope we can be forgiven for hastily sharing it.

Thank you to everyone who has submitted pictures, liked, shared and commented on Twitter, Facebook and Instagram. Your crockery crusade continues.

www.wewantplates.com
www.twitter.com/wewantplates
www.facebook.com/wewantplates
www.instagram.com/wewantplatesofficial

When a restaurant runs out of plates, grabbing the first flat thing to hand should not be an option.

A hollowed-out cricket bat, perfect for dispatching the food straight back to the kitchen.

Prawn cocktail served in a glass is fine. Prawn cocktail served in a glass on top of a live goldfish is not.

When the chef's late for work and nobody's emptied the dishwasher.

IRONING INSTRUCTIONS
Cotton: iron on high heat.
Silk: iron on medium heat.
Nylon: iron on low heat.
Prawns: iron on manky board.

Mini beef Wellingtons on barbed wire. That's just *perfect* for the dishwasher.

A well-organised kitchen is one thing, but serving food in an actual desk organiser is ridiculous.

Chefs! Transform sausages into more expensive sausages by putting them in a goth's ashtray!

Packet of pork scratchings: 89p.
Salad: 7p. Dip: 3p. Paper: 1p.
Hipster Pan Tax: £5.23.

'How would you like your lamb?'
'On a rock with two pairs of tweezers, please.'

Bloody Mary meatballs. The waiter didn't trip. They're actually supposed to look like that.

Wasabi sponge with a 'wow' factor. As in: 'Wow, some idiot has served my dinner on a tree.'

'Thanks for the ingredients to make my own tomato soup in a pan. Is there a DIY discount?'

What a load of pretentious scallops.

WE WANT PLATES

Somewhere, there's a confused pigeon looking for its nest. Unless he's in the starter.

On a positive note, it's been thoroughly washed for around 10,000 years.

'And how is the sea bass served?'
'In a tiny can, on a massive log.'
[*leaves*]

Centuries of plate smashing catches up with Greece as a crockery shortage leads to tzatziki/board woe.

A frankfurter martini.
[*peak hipster klaxon*]

Guillotine beef Wellingtons.
The chef's next up for the chop.

Is that ... is that actual salvage from a bathroom refit?

Shovel it down,
give it a wipe,
repeat.

WE WANT PLATES

You can't go wrong with a classic shepherd's pie. Unless you're the chef at this pub.

How to make a real dog's dinner of serving food to the public.

Because why wouldn't you serve lunch on a miniature skateboard at a Greek mineral spa full of pensioners?

'Pint of spaghetti bolognese?'
'Better not, I'm driving.'

This is what passes for fish and chips today. Fake fryer. Wooden board. Mushy peas and tartare sauce in mini milk churns.

'How are the **BBQ** prawns served?'
'On a tree with a ceramic rabbit.'
[*blinks*]

Lancashire hotpot.
That loud noise
you can hear is
Yorkshire laughing.

'I'm sorry our chef hasn't assembled your pulled pork burger, he's very busy buying artisanal slates online.'

Excellent chip-dam work to prevent a potential slate/sauce/trouser disaster.

Chicken in a basket. AN ACTUAL BASKET. Never seen the inside of a dishwasher and never will.

Answers on a postcard as to what purpose the mug serves.

'Wooden crate, metal bucket, tiny pan, fake fryer. Have we forgotten anything?' 'Taste, Chef?

[*dials 999*]
'Hello, what's your emergency?'
'I ordered a sandwich and it's
been served in a phone box.'

Literally scraping the bottom of the barrel.

Pizza boards are an exception to the rule, but in the case of this greasy old plank we applaud the note.

Just when you thought countryside tweeness couldn't get any worse than mini picnic benches ...

... they start serving lunch on mini country stiles.

When you order a cooked breakfast to cure a hangover but the sausage, egg, mushrooms and beans arrive in a tin and make you feel even worse.

Sausage and chips, as served to a three-year-old child. Things are about to get messy.

Presumably it's a record by Hot Chip.

'Chef, we're out of bread baskets.'
'Don't suppose you brought a
handbag to work, did you?'

Chefs! Make small portions look huge by serving them on tiny tables!

That feeling when you're recovering from the shock of chips being served in a glass and your corn on the cob arrives.

It's only a matter of time before we're all licking soup directly from waiters' cupped hands.

'FOUL SERVICE!'

Tapas in a teacup. Next door there's a quaint cafe serving Earl Grey in little terracotta dishes. They need to talk.

Remember the wheelie bin code: Green = garden waste. Black = cans and glass. Grey = overpriced crisps.

'DOWN IN ONE! DOWN IN ONE!'

Can't stand Russian dolls – they're just so full of themselves. Or pickles.

Macaroni Cauldron and Ketchup Syringe: a dish, not two obscure indie bands who supported Shed Seven in 1994.

Increasingly familiar 'bacon on a washing line' idiocy. Yes, this is now a thing.

WE WANT PLATES

**Sausages. In a tree.
A tree of sausages.
They served a tree
of sausages.**

'Wooooo! Spooky ghost cutlery!'
'We need to talk about your drinking, Chef.'

A valiant yet fruitless attempt to disguise the embarrassment of eating dessert from a tiny bath.

Chefs who serve pancakes and syrup on a wooden board with no gutter have clearly never waited tables.

'McDonald's on the way home?'
'Yep.'

The scourge of edible soil taken to the next level via the cheapest of plant pots and a slate. Best of luck keeping it off the table.

What happens if you like to save your ice cream until the end?

This is not a dessert. This is a round from *The Krypton Factor*.

Chocolate brownie and ice cream in a tankard. All kinds of wrongness.

A cake drawer. Perfect when dining with someone on the other side of the table whom you don't want to talk to.

Skateboard cheeseboard:
two words that should
never be seen together.

When you order a hot chocolate and what turns up screams: 'INFANTILIZE ME!'

Prosecco in an old welly.
We only gave them to the
charity shop last weekend!

The dishwasher's on the blink again.

'Would you like a can
for your ... erm ... can?'

Remember the good old days when a cocktail was just some nice booze in a glass?

At long last – **A PLATE!**
Shame they had to drink
out of a watering can
and bucket.

CONTRIBUTORS

A special thanks to all the contributors who provided photographs, without whom the book would not have been possible:

@MarinaOLoughlin, p. 5
@bobgranleese, p. 6
Rob Mackay, p. 8
@rugs77, pp. 12 and 58
@eeketht, p. 16
@JoWood04, p. 17
@SarahASculpher, p. 18
@millyandpip, p. 19
@braggken, p. 20
@Zahn0, p. 21
@AstridsTaste, p. 22
Mary Hudd, p. 23
@BrightSparkleJ, p. 24
@vinke_rob, p. 25
@hcbn, p. 26
@adwoolliscroft, p. 27
@SiMackie, p. 28
@butters_one, p. 29
@MirjamvD, p. 30
@NealP55, p. 31
@JAJRobertson, p. 32
  and front cover, bottom
@MJDoroszuk, p. 33
@Finlay_Johnson, p. 34
@simonraess, p. 35
@RichW82, p. 36
@kewgreen, p. 37
@positivedobba, p. 38
@followmartybear, p. 39
@johnnyhc, p. 40
@deanmorriscards, p. 41
@JayMeW, p. 44

@headcovers, p. 45
@zoecarrington, p. 46
@DJAFrankenstein, p. 47
@benhowell123, p. 48
@jill_wood, p. 49
@jamestaylor1, p. 50
@katebielinski, p. 51
@Sstenlake, p. 52
@SecEventsPen, p. 53
@neilwilley, p. 54
@Jlewisland, p. 55
@Cuff76, p. 56
@CrosbyTRobot, p. 57
@southsealmj, p. 59
@kjmci, p. 60
@simonjgray, p. 61
@vinayaravind, p. 62
@ashley_lyons08, p. 63
@Nick_Whittaker, p. 64
@StevePullan, p. 65
@jim_taylor, p. 66 and front
  cover, top right
@lone_smoggie, p. 67
@_paulhome, p. 68
@faulky5, p. 69
@littlednet, p. 72
@willdicki, p. 73 and front
  cover, top left
@83_baker, p. 74
@harrisphotog, p. 75
@thechocbakery, p. 76
@ILoveGrimsby, p. 77

@Alicechadfield, p. 78
@FrannyMontanny, p. 79
@helenium, p. 80
@StevoGDC, p. 81
@isobelblaikie, p. 82
Dan Paulston, p. 83
@SarahBridge100, p. 84
@GraysonThe, p. 85
@hldudley, p. 86
@9inelives, p. 87
@antbushell, p. 90
@MsDarlizzle, p. 91
@gavroche2000, p. 92
Linda Wilcock, p. 93
@simonr916, p. 94
@Ruthie_Ruth_, p. 95
@malarkey81, p. 96
@john_shepherd, p. 97
@Shrubshrub, p. 98
@boredjdc, p. 99
@ellespeller, p. 100
@Tannerlogue, p. 101
@Sleepypan, p. 104
@kittyroeactress, p. 105
@RobertOrdever, p. 106
@The_Hallissey, p. 107
@SmattStephenson, p. 108
@gavinj90, p. 109
@justandrea, p. 110
@deanna93, p. 111
Dawn Butler, back cover